Julia C. R. Dorr

Friar Anselmo

And Other Poems

Julia C. R. Dorr

Friar Anselmo
And Other Poems

ISBN/EAN: 9783744705431

Printed in Europe, USA, Canada, Australia, Japan

Cover: Foto ©Thomas Meinert / pixelio.de

More available books at **www.hansebooks.com**

FRIAR ANSELMO

AND OTHER POEMS,

BY
JULIA C. R. DORR.

NEW-YORK:
CHARLES SCRIBNER'S SONS.
1879.

CONTENTS.

	PAGE.
FRIAR ANSELMO	3
THE KING'S ROSEBUD	11
SOMEWHERE	13
A SECRET	14
PERADVENTURE	17
RENA—A LEGEND OF BRUSSELS	19
WHAT NEED?	35
THE KISS	37
WHAT SHE THOUGHT	39
THIS DAY	42
UNANSWERED	44
'CHRISTUS!"	48
THE CLAY TO THE ROSE	54
TWO	56
EVENTIDE	60
TO THE "BOUQUET CLUB"	63
AT THE LAST	65

CONTENTS.

	PAGE.
My Lovers	67
The Legend of the Organ-Builder	69
At Dawn	77
King Ivan's Oath	79
In Memoriam	89
Weaving the Web	91
Rabbi Benaiah	94
A Child's Thought	98
God Knows"	101
Unsolved	104
Five	109
Quietness	112
Winter	114
The "Christus" of Oberammergau	115
The Mountain Road	116
Entering In	119
The Difference	122
Thou Knowest	125
A Flower for the Dead	126
A Red Rose	129
My Birthday	131
Twenty-one	133
Thomas Moore (May 28, 1779—1879)	136
Singing in the Dark	139

CONTENTS.

SONNETS.

	PAGE.
TWO SONNETS. I.—II	141
TO ZÜLMA. I.—II	143
MERCÉDÈS	145
SLEEP	146
TO-DAY	147
GRASS-GROWN	148
AT THE TOMB	149
AT REST	150
F. A. F.	151
TOO WIDE!	152
RESURGAMUS	153
IN KING'S CHAPEL	154
THY NAME	155
THREE DAYS. I.—II.—III	156
VERMONT	159
A LAST WORD	177

TO S. M. D.

I BROUGHT thee, love, the first pale buds of spring,
   Frail blooms that trembled in the lonely dells;
   Wild violets, mayhap, or nodding bells
Gathered when happy birds on joyous wing
Fluttered from bough to bough to coo and sing.
   I brought thee summer roses, such as grow
   In our own garden ground, and do not know
The grace of tenderer culture. Now I bring
The early flowers of autumn — golden-rod
   Plucked by the wayside, asters starry-eyed,
   With here and there, alas! a crimson leaf
That dropped, untimely, on the waiting sod.
   Dear heart! refuse not thou this later sheaf
   From fields where we have wandered side by side.

"The Maples," September, 1879.

FRIAR ANSELMO.

FRIAR ANSELMO.

FRIAR ANSELMO for a secret sin
  Sat bowed with grief the convent cell within;
Nor dared, such was his shame, to lift his eyes
To the low wall whereon, in dreadful guise,
The dead CHRIST hung upon the cursèd tree,
Frowning, he thought, upon his misery.
What was his sin it matters not to tell.
  But he was young and strong, the records say;
Perhaps he wearied of his narrow cell;
  Perhaps he longed to work, as well as pray;
  Perhaps his heart too warmly beat that day!
Perhaps—for life is long—the weary road
That he must travel, bearing as a load
The slow, monotonous hours that, one by one,
Dragged in a lengthening chain from sun to sun,
Appalled his eager spirit, and his vow
Pressed like an iron hand upon his brow.
Perhaps some dream of love, of home, of wife,
Had stirred this tumult in his lonely life,

Tempting his soul to barter heavenly bliss,
And sell its birthright for a woman's kiss!
At all events, the struggle had been hard;
And as a bird from the glad ether barred,
So had he beat his wings till, bruised and torn,
He wished that night he never had been born!
And still the dead CHRIST on the cursèd tree
Seemed but to mock his hopeless misery;
Still Mary mother turned her eyes away,
Nor saint nor angel bent to hear him pray!

The calm, cold moonlight through the casement shone;
Weird shadows darkened on the floor of stone;
Without, what solemn splendors! and within
What fearful wrestlings with despair and sin!
Sudden and loud the cloister bell outrang;
Afar a door swung to with sullen clang;
And overhead he heard the rhythmic beat,
The measured monotone of many feet
Seeking the chapel for the midnight prayer.
Black wings seemed hovering round him in the air,
Beating him back as with a stifled moan

He would have sought the holy altar stone.
Then with a swift, sharp cry, prostrate he fell
Before the crucifix. "The gates of hell
Shall not prevail against me!" loud he cried,
Stretching his arms to CHRIST, the crucified.
"By Thy dread cross, Thy dying agony,
Thine awful passion, LORD, deliver me!"

Was it a dream? The taunting demons fled;
Through the dim cell a wondrous glory spread;
And all the air was filled with rare perfumes
Wafted from censers rich with heavenly blooms.
Transfigured stood the CHRIST before his eyes,
Clothed in white samite, woven in Paradise,
And from the empty cross upon the wall
Streamed a wide splendor that encompassed all!
Was it a dream? Anselmo's sight grew dim;
The cloistered chamber seemed to reel and swim;
Yet well his spirit knew the glorious guest,
And all his manhood rose to meet the test.
"What wilt Thou have me, LORD, to do?" he cried
  With pallid lips, and kissed the sacred feet.

And then in accents strangely calm, yet sweet,
These words he heard from CHRIST, the crucified,
The pitying CHRIST his inmost soul who read,
With all its wild unrest, its doubt and dread:
"MAKE THOU A COPY OF MY HOLY WORD!"
Then mystic presences about him stirred;
The vision faded. At the dawn of day
Prostrate and pallid in the dusk he lay.
Was it a dream? GOD knows! The narrow cell
Wore the old aspect he had learned so well,
And from the crucifix upon the wall
No glory streamed illuminating all!
Yet still a subtile fragrance filled the room;
And looking round him in the soft, gray gloom,
Anselmo saw upon the fretted floor
An eagle's quill that this grave legend bore:
"He works most nobly for his fellow-men
Who gives My word to them, by tongue or pen!"

Henceforth Anselmo prayed, but worked as well,
Nor felt the bondage of his cloister cell;
For all his soul was filled with high intent,

He had no dream save its accomplishment —
To make a copy of the Holy Word,
Fairer than eye had seen, or ear had heard,
Or heart conceived of! Day by day he wrought,
His fingers guided by a single thought;
Forming each letter with the tenderest care,
With points of richest color here and there;
With birds on swaying boughs, and butterflies
   Poised on gay wings o'er sprays of eglantine;
   With tangled tracery of flower and vine
   Through which gleamed cherub faces, half divine;
With fading leaves that drift when Summer dies,
And angels floating down the evening skies —
Each word an orison, each line a prayer!
Slowly the work went on from day to day;
The seasons came and went; May followed May;
Year after year passed by with stately tread
To join the countless legions of the dead,
Till Fra Anselmo, wan and bowed with age,
Bent, a gray monk, above the parchment page.
Death waited till he wrote the last fair line,
Then touched his hand and closed the Book Divine!

POEMS.

THE KING'S ROSEBUD.

ONLY a blushing rosebud, folding up
  Such wealth of sweetness in its dewy cup
That the whole air was like rare incense flung
From golden censers round high altars swung!
One day the king passed by with stately tread,
And, reaching forth his hand, he lightly said,
"All sweets are mine; therefore this rose I take,
And wear it in my bosom for Love's sake."
Then, while the king passed on with smiling face,
The sweet rose gloried in its pride of place.

But ah! the deeds that in Love's name are done!
The woeful wrack wrought underneath the sun!
Still with that smile upon his lip, the king
Laid his rash hand upon the beauteous thing;

In hot haste tore the crimson leaves apart,
And drained the sweetness from its glowing heart;
Seared the soft petals with his fiery breath,
Then tossed it from him to ignoble death!
When next with idle steps I passed that way,
Prone in the mire the king's fair rosebud lay.

SOMEWHERE.

How can I cease to pray for thee? Somewhere
   In God's great universe thou art to-day:
Can He not reach thee with His tender care?
   Can He not hear me when for thee I pray?

What matters it to Him who holds within
   The hollow of His hand all worlds, all space,
That thou art done with earthly pain and sin?
   Somewhere within His ken thou hast a place.

Somewhere thou livest and hast need of Him:
   Somewhere thy soul sees higher heights to climb;
And somewhere still there may be valleys dim
   That thou must pass to reach the hills sublime.

Then all the more, because thou canst not hear
   Poor human words of blessing, will I pray,
O true, brave heart! God bless thee, wheresoe'er
   In His great universe thou art to-day!

A SECRET.

It is your secret and mine, love!
   Ah, me! how the dreary rain
With a slow persistence, all day long
   Dropped on the window pane!
The chamber was weird with shadows
   And dark with the deepening gloom
Where you, in your royal womanhood,
   Lay waiting for the tomb.

They had robed you all in white, love;
   In your hair was a single rose—
A marble rose it might well have been
   In its cold and still repose!

A SECRET.

O, paler than yonder carven saint,
   And calm as the angels are,
You seemed so near me, my beloved,
   Yet were, alas, so far!

I do not know if I wept, love;
   But my soul rose up and said,—
"My heart shall speak unto her heart,
   Though here she is lying—dead!
I will give her a last love-token
   That shall be to her a sign
In the dark grave—or beyond it!—
   Of this deathless love of mine.

So I sought me a little scroll, love;
   And thereon, in eager haste,
Lest another's eye should read them
   Some mystic words I traced.
Then close in your claspèd fingers,
   Close in your waxen hand,
I placed the scroll for an amulet,
   Sure you would understand!

A SECRET.

The secret is yours and mine, love!
   Only we two may know
What words shine clear in the darkness,
   Of your grave so green and low.
But if when we meet hereafter,
   In the dawn of some fairer day,
You whisper those mystical words, love,
   It is all I would have you say!

PERADVENTURE.

I AM thinking to-night of the little child
  That lay on my breast three summer days,
Then swiftly, silently, dropped from sight,
  While my soul cried out in sore amaze.

It is fifteen years ago to-night;
  Somewhere, I know, he has lived them through,
Perhaps with never a thought or dream
  Of the mother-heart he never knew!

Is he yet but a babe? or has he grown
  To be like his brothers, fair and tall,
With a clear bright eye, and a springing step,
  And a voice that rings like a bugle call?

I loved him. The rose in his waxen hand
  Was wet with the dew of my falling tears;

I have kept the thought of my baby's grave
　　Through all the length of these changeful years.

Yet the love I gave him was not like that
　　I give to-day to my other boys,
Who have grown beside me, and turned to me
　　In all their griefs and in all their joys.

Do you think he knows it? I wonder much
　　If the dead are passionless, cold and dumb;
If into the calm of the deathless years
　　No thrill of a human love may come!

Perhaps sometimes from the upper air
　　He has seen me walk with his brothers three;
Or felt in the tender twilight hour
　　The breath of the kisses they gave to me!

Over his birthright, lost so soon,
　　Perhaps he has sighed as the swift years flew;
O child of my heart! you shall find somewhere
　　The love that on earth you never knew!

RENA.

(A LEGEND OF BRUSSELS.)

I.

St. Gudula's bells were chiming for the midnight, sad and slow,
In the ancient town of Brussels, many and many a year ago,

And St. Michael, poised so grandly on his lofty, airy height,
Seemed transfigured in the glory of the full moon's tender light,

When, a fair and saintly maiden, crowned with locks of palest gold,
Rena stood beside her lover, son of Hildebrand the Bold.

She with grief and tears was pallid; but his face was
    hard and stern:
All the passion of his being in his dark eyes seemed
    to burn.

"Never dream that I will give thee back thy plighted
    faith," he cried,
"By St. Michael's sword I swear it, thou, my love,
    shalt be my bride!"

"Nay, but hear me," she responded; "hear the
    words that I must speak;
I must speak, and thou must hearken, though my
    heart is like to break.

"Yestermorn, as I sat spinning blithely at my cot-
    tage door,
Straightway fell a stately shadow in the sunshine on
    the floor;

"And a figure stood before me, so majestic and so
    grand,

That I knew it in a moment for the mighty Hildebrand;—

"Stood and gazed on me till downward at my feet the distaff dropped,
And in all my veins the pulsing of the swift life-current stopped.

"'Thou art Rena,' then he uttered, and he swore a dreadful oath,
And the tempest of his anger beat on me and on us both.

"'She who thinks to wed with Volmar must have lands and gold,' said he,
'Or must come of noble lineage, fit to mate with mine and me!

"'Thou art but a peasant maiden, empty-handed, lowly born;
All the ladies of my castle would look down on thee with scorn.

"' Even he will weary of thee when his passion once is spent,
Vainly cursing her who doomed him to an endless discontent!'

"Then I, trembling, rose up slowly, and I looked him in the face,
Though the dreadful frown it wore seemed to darken all the place.

"' Sir, I thank you for this warning,' said I, speaking low and clear,
'But the laughter of your ladies I must teach my heart to bear.

"' For the rest — your son is noble — and my simple womanhood'
He will hold in loving honor, as a saint the holy rood!'

"Oh! then his stern face whitened, and a bitter laugh laughed he:

'Truly this my son is noble, and he shall not wed
    with thee.

"'Hear my words now, and remember! for by this
    good sword I swear,
And by Michael standing yonder, watching us from
    upper air,

"'If he dares to place a wedding-ring upon your
    dowerless hand,
On his head shall fall a father's curse—the curse of
    Hildebrand!'

"O, my Volmar! Then the earth rocked, and I fell
    down in a swoon;
When I woke the room was silent; it was past the
    hour of noon;

"And I waited for thy coming, as the captive waits
    for death,
With a mingled dread and longing, and a half-abated
    breath!"

Straight the young man bowed before her, as before
    a holy shrine :
"Never hand of high-born lady was more richly
    dowered than thine!

"What care I for gold or honors, or — my — father's
    — curse?" he said;
But the words died out in shudders, and his face
    grew like the dead.

Then she twined her white arms round him, and she
    murmured, sweet and low,
As the night wind breathing softly over banks where
    violets blow:

"'He who is accursed of father, he shall be accursed
    of God,'
Long ago said one who followed where the holy
    prophets trod.

"Kiss me once, then, O my Volmar! just once more,
    my Volmar dear,

Even as you would kiss my white lips if I lay upon
  my bier!

"For a gulf as dark as death has opened wide 'twixt
  thee and me;
Neither thou nor I can cross it, and thy wife I may
  not be!"

II.

ONCE again the bells of midnight chimed from St.
  Gudula's towers,
While St. Michael watched the city slumbering through
  the ghostly hours.

But no slumber came to Rena where she moaned in
  bitter pain,
For the anguish of that parting wrought its work on
  heart and brain.

Suddenly the air grew heavy as with magical per-
  fume,

And a weird and wondrous splendor filled the dim and silent room.

In the middle of the chamber stood a lady fair and sweet,
With bright tresses falling softly to her small and sandaled feet.

Flushed her cheeks were as a wild rose, and the glory of her eyes
Was the laughing light and glory of the kindling morning skies.

Airy robes of lightest tissue from her white arms floated free;
They seemed woven of the mist that curls above the azure sea,

Wrought in curious devices, star and wheel and leaf and flower,
That, like frost upon a window-pane, might vanish in an hour.

In her hands she bore a cushion, quaintly fashioned, strangely set
With small silver pins that spanned it like a branching coronet;

And from threads of finest texture swung light bobbins to and fro,
As the lady stood illumined in the weird and wondrous glow.

Not a single word she uttered; but, as silent as a shade,
Down the room she swiftly glided and beside the startled maid

Knelt, a radiant vision, smiling into Rena's wondering eyes,
Giving arch yet gracious answer to her tremulous surprise.

Then she laid the satin cushion on the wondering maiden's knee,

And to all her mute bewilderment, no syllable spake she.

But, as in and out and round about, the silver pins among,
Flashed the white hand of the lady, and the shining bobbins swung,

Lo! a web of fairy lightness like the misty robe she wore,
Swiftly grew beneath her fingers, drifting downward to the floor!

And as Rena looked and wondered, inch by inch the marvel grew,
Till the eastern windows brightened as the gray dawn struggled through.

Then the lady's hand touched Rena's, and she pointed far away,
Where the palace towers were gleaming in the first red light of day.

But when once again the maiden turned her glance within the room,
With the lady fair had vanished all the splendor and perfume.

Still the satin cushion lay there, quaintly fashioned, strangely set
With the silver pins that spanned it like a branching coronet;

Still the light web she had woven lay in drifts upon the floor,
Like the mist wreaths resting softly on some lone, enchanted shore!

III.

Slowly Rena raised the cushion, with her sweet eyes shining clear,
Lightly tossed the fairy bobbins, half in gladness, half in fear.

Ah! not vain had been her watching as the lovely lady wrought;
All the magic of her fingers her own cunning hand had caught!

Many a day above the cushion Rena's peerless head was bent,
And through many a solemn night she labored on with sweet intent.

For, mayhap, the mystic marvels that she wove might bring her gold—
A fair dowry fit to match the pride of Hildebrand the Bold!

Then she braided up her long hair, and put on her russet gown,
And with wicker basket laden passed she swiftly through the town,

To the palace where Queen Ildegar, with dames of high degree,

In a lofty oriel window sat, the beauteous morn to see.

In the door-way she stood meekly, till the queen said, " Maiden fair,
What have you in yonder basket that you carry with such care ? "

Eagerly she raised her blue eyes, hovering smiles and tears between,
Then across the room she glided, and knelt down before the queen.

Lifting up the wicker cover, " Saints in heaven ! " cried Ildegar,
" Here are tissues fit for angels, wrought with wreath and point and star,

" In most curious devices ! Never saw I aught so rare—
Where found you these frail webs woven of the lightest summer air ? "

"Well they may be fit for angels," said she, underneath her breath;
"O my lady, hear a story that is strange and true as death."

But ere yet the tale was ended, up rose good Queen Ildegar,
And she sent her knights and pages to the castle riding far.

"Bring me Hildebrand and Volmar, ere the sun goes down!" she cried,
"Ho! my ladies, for a wedding, and your queen shall bless the bride!

"I will buy these airy wonders, and this maiden in her hand
Shall a dowry hold as royal as the noblest in the land."

So they combed her shining tresses, and they brought her robes of silk,

Broidered thick with gold and silver, on a ground as white as milk.

But she whispered, "Sweetest ladies, let me wear my russet gown,
That I wore this happy morning walking blithely through the town.

"I am but a peasant maiden, all unused to grand estate,
And for robes of silken splendor, dearest ladies, let me wait!"

Then the good queen, smiling brightly, from the wicker basket took
Lightest web of quaintest pattern, and its filmy folds outshook.

With her own white hand she laid it over Rena's golden hair,
And she cried, "Oh, look, my ladies! Ne'er before was bride so fair!"

5

Ladies! when you wear your Brussels laces, costlier
    far than gold,
Think of Rena, and her lover, son of Hildebrand
    the Bold!

WHAT NEED?

" What need has the singer to sing?
  And why should your poet to-day
His pale little garland of poesy bring,
    On the altar to lay?
High-priests of song the harp-strings swept
Ages before he smiled or wept!"

What need have the roses to bloom?
  And why do the tall lilies grow?
And why do the violets shed their perfume
    When night-winds breathe low?
They are no whit more bright and fair
Than flowers that breathed in Eden's air!

What need have the stars to shine on?
  Or the clouds to grow red in the west,
When the sun, like a king, from the fields he has won,
    Goes grandly to rest?
No brighter they than stars and skies
That greeted Eve's sweet, wondering eyes!

WHAT NEED?

What need has the eagle to soar
   So proudly straight up to the sun?
Or the robin such jubilant music to pour
      When day is begun?
The eagles soared, the robins sung,
As high, as sweet, when earth was young!

What need, do you ask me? Each day
   Hath a song and a prayer of its own,
As each June hath its crown of fresh roses, each May
      Its bright emerald throne!
Its own high thought each age shall stir,
Each needs its own interpreter!

And thou, O, my poet, sing on!
   Sing on until love shall grow old;
Till patience and faith their last triumphs have won,
      And truth is a tale that is told!
Doubt not, thy song shall still be new
While life endures and God is true!

THE KISS.

When you lay before me dead,
 In such pallid rest,
On those passive lips of thine
 Not one kiss I pressed!

Did you wonder—looking down
 From some higher sphere—
Knowing how we two had loved
 Many and many a year?

Did you think me strange and cold
 When I did not touch,
Even with reverent finger-tips,
 What I had loved so much?

Ah! when last you kissed me, dear,
 Know you what you said?

THE KISS.

"Take this last kiss, my beloved,
  Soon shall I be dead!

"Keep it for a solemn sign,
  Through our love's long night,
Till you give it back again
  On some morning bright."

So I gave you no caress;
  But, remembering this,
Warm upon my lips I keep
  Your last living kiss!

WHAT SHE THOUGHT.

MARION showed me her wedding gown
   And her veil of gossamer lace to-night,
And the orange-blooms that to-morrow morn
   Shall fade in her soft hair's golden light.
But Philip came to the open door:
   Like the heart of a wild-rose glowed her cheek,
And they wandered off through the garden paths
   So blest that they did not care to speak.

I wonder how it seems to be loved;
   To know you are fair in some one's eyes;
That upon some one your beauty dawns
   Every day as a new surprise;
To know, that, whether you weep or smile,
   Whether your mood be grave or gay,
Somebody thinks you, all the while,
   Sweeter than any flower of May.

WHAT SHE THOUGHT.

I wonder what it would be to love:
    That, I think, would be sweeter far,
To know that one out of all the world
    Was lord of your life, your king, your star.
They talk of love's sweet tumult and pain:
    I am not sure that I understand,
Though—a thrill ran down to my finger-tips
    Once when—somebody—touched my hand!

I wonder what it would be to dream
    Of a child that might one day be your own;
Of the hidden springs of your life a part,
    Flesh of your flesh, and bone of your bone.
Marion stooped one day to kiss
    A beggar's babe with a tender grace;
While some sweet thought, like a prophecy,
    Looked from her pure Madonna face.

I wonder what it must be to think
    To-morrow will be your wedding-day,
And you, in the radiant sunset glow
    Down fragrant flowery paths will stray,

As Marion does this blessed night,
  With Philip, lost in a blissful dream.
Can she feel his heart through the silence beat?
  Does he see her eyes in the starlight gleam?

Questioning thus, my days go on;
  But never an answer comes to me:
All love's mysteries, sweet as strange,
  Sealed away from my life must be.
Yet still I dream, O heart of mine!
  Of a beautiful city that lies afar;
And there, some time, I shall drop the mask,
  And be shapely and fair as others are.

THIS DAY.

I WONDER what is this day to you,
  Looking down from the upper skies!
Is there a pang at your gentle heart?
  Is there a shade in your tender eyes?
Do you think up there of the whispered words
  That thrilled your soul in the long ago?
Does ever a haunting undertone
  Blend with the chantings sweet and low?

When this day dawned (if where you are
  Skies grow red when the morn is near)
Did you know that before its close
  The love once yours would be on its bier?
Did you know that another's lip
  Would redden with kisses once your own,
And the golden cup of a younger life
  O'erflow with the wine once yours alone?

THIS DAY.

Do you remember? Ah! my saint,
    Bend your ear from the ether blue!
Have you risen to heights so far
    That earth and its loves are nought to you?
Do you care that your place is filled?
    Does it matter that now at last
The turf above you has grown so deep
    That its shadow overlies your past?

O, belovèd, I may not know!
    Heaven is afar, and the grave is dumb,
And out of the silence so profound
    Neither token nor voice may come!
We try to think that we understand;
    But whether you wake, or whether you sleep,
Or whether our deeds are aught to you,
    Is still a mystery strange and deep!

UNANSWERED.

Where mountain-peaks rose far and high
Into the blue, unclouded sky,
And waves of green, like billowy seas,
Tossed proudly in the freshening breeze,

I rode one morning, late in June.
The glad winds sang a pleasant tune;
The air, like draughts of rarest wine,
Made every breath a joy divine.

With roses all the way was bright;
Yet there upon that upland height
The darlings of the early spring—
Blue violets—were blossoming.

And all the meadows, wide unrolled,
Were green and silver, green and gold,

UNANSWERED.

Where buttercups and daisies spun
Their shining tissues in the sun.

Over its shallow, pebbly bed,
A sparkling river gayly sped,
Nor cared that deeper waters bore
A grander freight from shore to shore.

It sung, it danced, it laughed, it played,
In sunshine now and now in shade;
While every gnarled tree joyed to make
A greener garland for its sake.

Deep peace was in the summer air,
A peace all Nature seemed to share;
Yet even there I could not flee
The shadow of life's mystery!

A farm-house stood beside the way,
Low-roofed and rambling, quaint and gray;
And where the friendly door swung wide
Red roses climbed on either side.

And thither, down the winding road
Near which the sparkling river flowed,
In groups, in pairs, the neighbors pressed,
Each in his Sunday raiment dressed.

A sober calm was on each face;
Sweet stillness brooded o'er the place;
Yet something of a festal air
The youths and maidens seemed to wear.

But, as I passed, an idle breeze
Swept through the quivering maple-trees;
Chased by the winds in merry rout,
A fair, light curtain floated out.

And this I saw: a quiet room
Adorned with flowers of richest bloom—
A lily here, a garland there—
Fragrance and silence everywhere.

Then on I rode. But if a bride
Should there her happy blushes hide,

UNANSWERED.

Or if beyond my vision lay
Some pale face shrouded from the day,

I could not tell. O Joy and Pain,
Your voices join in one refrain!
So like ye are, we may not know
If this be gladness, this be woe!

"CHRISTUS!"

Over the desolate sea-side town
With a terrible tumult the night came down,
And the fierce wind swept through the empty street,
With the drifting snow for a winding-sheet.
Elsie, the fisherman's daughter, in bed
Lay and listened in awe and dread,
But sprang to her feet in sudden fear
When over the tempest, loud and clear,
    A voice cried, " Christus!"

" Christus! Christus!" and nothing more.
Was it a cry at the cottage-door?
She left her chamber with flying feet;
She loosened the bolts with fingers fleet;
She lifted the latch, but only the din

Of the furious storm and the snow swept in.
She looked without: not a soul was there,
But still rang out on the startled air
      The strange cry, "Christus!"

"Christus! Christus!" She slept at last,
Though the old house rocked in the wintry blast;
And when she awoke the world was still,
A wide, white silence from sea to hill.
No creature stirred in the morning glow;
There was not a footprint in the snow;
Yet again through the hush, as faint and far
As if it came from another star,
      A voice sighed, "Christus!"

"Christus! Christus!" Who can it be,
O Christ our Lord, that is calling Thee
In a foreign tongue, with a woe as wild
As that of some lost, forsaken child?
She turned from the window with startled gaze:
She clasped her hands in a pale amaze,
Hearkening still, till again she heard,

As in a waking dream, the word—
    That strange word, "Christus!"

Then over the hill with weary feet
She toiled through the drifts to the village-street.
The villagers gathered in eager haste,
And all day long in the snowy waste
They sought in vain for the one who cried
To Him who of old was crucified:
Then, turning away with a laugh, they said,
"'T was only the wild wind overhead,
    Your cry of 'Christus!'"

She watched their going with earnest eyes:
Hark! what voice to the taunt replies?
The trees were still as if struck with death;
The wind was soft as a baby's breath;
The sobbing sea was asleep at last,
Scourged no more by the furious blast;
Yet, surely as ever from human tongue
A cry of grief or despair was wrung,
    Some voice sighed, "Christus!"

"CHRISTUS!"

Burned on her cheek a sudden flame
As her heart's strong throbbings went and came,
And she stood alone on the lonely shore,
Gazing the wide black waters o'er.
"Whether it comes from heaven or hell,
This voice I have learned to know too well—
Whether from lips alive or dead,
Or from the hovering air," she said—
"Whether it comes from sea or land,
I will not sleep till I understand
    This cry of 'Christus!'"

"Christus! Christus!" Faint and slow
Rose the wail from the drifted snow
Under a low-browed, beetling rock,
Strong to withstand the whirlwind's shock.
There, in the heart of the snowy mound,
The buried form of a man she found—
A Spanish sailor, with beard of brown
Over his red scarf flowing down,
And jeweled ears that were strange to see.
She was bending over it, when—ah me!—
    The shrill cry, "Christus!"

Rang out as if from the stony lips
Whence life had parted in drear eclipse,
As if the soul of the dead man cried
Again unto Christ the Crucified.
The rose had fled from her cheeks so red,
But still she knelt by his side and said,
Under her breath, " I must understand
Whether from heaven or sea or land
   Comes that cry, ' Christus ! ' "

She laid her hand on the pulseless breast:
What fluttered beneath the crimson vest?
A bird with plumage of green and gold,
Nestling away from the piercing cold,
Was folded close to the silent heart
From which it had felt the life depart;
And when she held it against her cheek,
As plainly as ever a bird could speak
   It sobbed out, " Christus ! "

And evermore when the winds blew loud,
And the trees in the grasp of the storm were bowed,

And the lowering wings of the tempest beat
The drifting snow in the village-street,
Just as its master in death had cried
To Christ, the Holy, the Crucified,
Pouring his soul in one wild word—
Pray God that the cry in heaven was heard!—
    The bird cried, "Christus!"

THE CLAY TO THE ROSE.

O BEAUTIFUL, royal Rose,
    O Rose, so fair and sweet!
Queen of the garden art thou,
    And I—the Clay at thy feet!

The butterfly hovers about thee;
    The brown bee kisses thy lips;
And the humming-bird, reckless rover,
    Their marvelous sweetness sips.

The sunshine hastes to caress thee
    Flying on pinions fleet;
The dew-drop sleeps in thy bosom,
    But I—I lie at thy feet!

The radiant morning crowns thee;
    And the noon's hot heart is thine;

THE CLAY TO THE ROSE.

And the starry night enfolds thee
   In the might of its love divine;

I hear the warm rain whisper
   Its message soft and sweet;
And the south-wind's passionate murmur,
   While I lie low at thy feet!

It is not mine to approach thee;
   I never may kiss thy lips,
Or touch the hem of thy garment
   With tremulous finger-tips.

Yet, O thou beautiful Rose!
   Queen rose, so fair and sweet,
What were lover or crown to thee
   Without the Clay at thy feet?

TWO.

We two will stand in the shadow here,
    To see the bride as she passes by;
Ring soft and low, ring loud and clear,
    Ye chiming bells that swing on high!
Look! look! she comes! The air grows sweet
    With the fragrant breath of the orange blooms,
And the flowers she treads beneath her feet
    Die in a flood of rare perfumes!

She comes! she comes! The happy bells
    With their joyous clamor fill the air,
While the great organ dies and swells,
    Soaring to trembling heights of prayer!
Oh! rare are her robes of silken sheen,
    And the pearls that gleam on her bosom's snow;
But rarer the grace of her royal mien,
    Her hair's fine gold, and her cheek's young glow.

TWO.

Dainty and fair as a folded rose,
   Fresh as a violet dewy sweet,
Chaste as a lily, she hardly knows
   That there are rough paths for other feet.
For Love hath shielded her; Honor kept
   Watch beside her by night and day;
And Evil out from her sight hath crept,
   Trailing its slow length far away.

Now in her perfect womanhood,
   In all the wealth of her matchless charms,
Lovely and beautiful, pure and good,
   She yields herself to her lover's arms.
Hark! how the jubilant voices ring!
   Lo! as we stand in the shadow here,
While far above us the gay bells swing,
   I catch the gleam of a happy tear!

The pageant is over. Come with me
   To the other side of the town, I pray,
Ere the sun goes down in the darkening sea,
   And night falls around us, chill and gray.

In the dim church porch an hour ago,
    We waited the bride's fair face to see;
Now Life has a sadder sight to show,
    A darker picture for you and me.

No need to seek for the shadow here;
    There are shadows lurking everywhere;
These streets in the brightest day are drear,
    And black as the blackness of despair.
But this is the house. Take heed, my friend,
    The stairs are rotten, the way is dim;
And up the flights, as we still ascend,
    Creep stealthy phantoms dark and grim.

Enter this chamber. Day by day,
    Alone in this chill and ghostly room,
A child—a woman—which is it, pray?—
    Despairingly waits for the hour of doom!
Ah! as she wrings her hands so pale,
    No gleam of a wedding ring you see;
There is nothing to tell. You know the tale—
    God help her now in her misery!

TWO.

I dare not judge her. I only know
   That love was to her a sin and a snare,
While to the bride of an hour ago
   It brought all blessings its hands could bear!
I only know that to one it came
   Laden with honor, and joy, and peace:
Its gifts to the other were woe and shame,
   And a burning pain that shall never cease!

I only know that the soul of one
   Has been a pearl in a golden case;
That of the other a pebble thrown
   Idly down in a way-side place,
Where all day long strange footsteps trod,
   And the bold, bright sun drank up the dew!
Yet both were women. O righteous God,
   Thou only canst judge between the two!

EVENTIDE.

Whenever, with reverent footsteps,
  I pass through the mystic door
Of Memory's stately palace,
  Where dwell the days of yore,
One scene, like a lovely vision,
  Comes to me o'er and o'er.

'T is a dim, fire-lighted chamber;
  There are pictures on the wall,
And around them dance the shadows
  Grotesque and weird and tall,
As the flames on the storied hearth-stone
  Wavering rise and fall.

An ancient cabinet stands there,
  That came from beyond the seas,
With a breath of spicy odors

Caught from the Indian breeze;
And its fluted doors and moldings
  Are dark with mysteries.

There's an old arm-chair in the corner,
  Straight-backed and tall and quaint;
Ah! many a generation—
  Sinner and sage and saint—
It hath held in its ample bosom
  With murmur nor complaint!

In the glow of the fire-light playing,
  A tiny, blithesome pair,
With the music of their laughter
  Fill all the tranquil air,—
A rosy, brown-eyed lassie,
  A boy serenely fair.

A woman sits in the shadow
  Watching the children twain,
With a joy so deep and tender
  It is near akin to pain,

And a smile and tear blend softly—
   Sunshine and April rain!

Her heart keeps time to the rhythm
   Of love's unuttered prayer,
As, with still hands lightly folded,
   She listens, unaware,
Through all the children's laughter,
   For a footfall on the stair.

I know the woman who sits there;
   Time hath been kind to her,
And the years have brought her treasures
   Of frankincense and myrrh
Richer, perhaps, and rarer,
   Than Life's young roses were.

But I doubt if ever her spirit
   Hath known, or yet shall know,
The bliss of a happier hour,
   As the swift years come and go,
Than this in the shadowy chamber
   Lit by the hearth-fire's glow!

TO THE "BOUQUET CLUB."

O ROSEBUD garland of girls!
   Who ask for a song from me,
To what sweet air shall I set my lay?
   What shall its key-note be?
The flowers have gone from wood and hill;
The rippling river lies white and still;
And the bird that sang on the maple bough,
Afar in the South-land singeth now!

O Rosebud garland of girls!
   If the whole glad year were May;
If winds sang low in the clustering leaves,
   And roses bloomed alway;
If youth were all that there is of life;
If the years brought nothing of care or strife,
Nor even a cloud to the ether blue,
It were easy to sing a song for you!

Yet, O my garland of girls!
   Is there nothing better than May?
The golden glow of the harvest time!
   The rest of the Autumn day!
This thought I give to you all to keep:
Who soweth good seed shall surely reap;
The year grows rich as it groweth old,
And life's latest sands are its sands of gold!

AT THE LAST.

Will the day ever come, I wonder,
   When I shall be glad to know
That my hands will be folded under
   The next white fall of the snow?
To know that when next the clover
   Wooeth the wandering bee,
Its crimson tide will drift over
   All that is left of me?

Will I ever be tired of living,
   And be glad to go to my rest,
With a cool and fragrant lily
   Asleep on my silent breast?
Will my eyes grow weary of seeing,
   As the hours pass, one by one,
Till I long for the hush and the darkness
   As I never longed for the sun?

God knoweth! Sometime, it may be,
    I shall smile to hear you say:
"Dear heart! she will not waken
    At the dawn of another day!"
And sometime, love, it may be,
    I shall whisper under my breath:
"The happiest hour of my life, dear,
    Is this — the hour of my death!"

MY LOVERS.

I have four noble lovers,
   Young and gallant, blithe and gay,
And in all the land no maiden
   Hath a goodlier troupe than they!
And never princess, guarded
   By knights of high degree,
Knew sweeter, purer homage
   Than my lovers pay to me!

One of my noble lovers
   Is a self-poised, thoughtful man,
Gravely gay, serenely earnest,
   Strong to do, and bold to plan!
And one is sweet and sunny,
   Pure as crystal, true as steel,
With a soul responding ever
   When the truth makes high appeal!

MY LOVERS.

And another of my lovers,
   Bright and *debonair* is he,
Brave and ardent, strong and tender,
   And the flower of courtesie!
Last of all, an eager student,
   Upon lofty aims intent:
Manly force and gentle sweetness
   In his nature rarely blent!

But when of noble lovers
   All alike are dear and true,
And her heart to choose refuses,
   Pray, what can a woman do?
Ah, my sons! For this I bless ye,
   Even as I myself am blest,
That I know not which is dearest,
   That I care not which is best!

THE LEGEND OF THE ORGAN-BUILDER.

Day by day the Organ-Builder in his lonely chamber wrought;
Day by day the soft air trembled to the music of his thought;

Till at last the work was ended, and no organ voice so grand
Ever yet had soared responsive to the master's magic hand.

Ay, so rarely was it builded that whenever groom or bride
Who in God's sight were well-pleasing in the church stood side by side,

Without touch or breath the organ of itself began to play,

And the very airs of heaven through the soft gloom
    seemed to stray.

He was young, the Organ-Builder, and o'er all the
    land his fame
Ran with fleet and eager footsteps, like a swiftly
    rushing flame.

All the maidens heard the story; all the maidens
    blushed and smiled,
By his youth and wondrous beauty and his great
    renown beguiled.

So he sought and won the fairest, and the wedding
    day was set:
Happy day — the brightest jewel in the glad year's
    coronet!

But when they the portal entered, he forgot his
    lovely bride —
Forgot his love, forgot his God, and his heart
    swelled high with pride.

"Ah!" thought he, "how great a master am I! When the organ plays,
How the vast cathedral arches will re-echo with my praise!"

Up the aisle the gay procession moved. The altar shone afar,
With its every candle gleaming through soft shadows like a star.

But he listened, listened, listened, with no thought of love or prayer,
For the swelling notes of triumph from his organ standing there.

All was silent. Nothing heard he save the priest's low monotone,
And the bride's robe trailing softly o'er the floor of fretted stone.

Then his lips grew white with anger. Surely God was pleased with him

Who had built the wondrous organ for His temple
 vast and dim?

Whose the fault, then? Hers—the maiden standing
 meekly at his side!
Flamed his jealous rage, maintaining she was false
 to him—his bride.

Vain were all her protestations, vain her innocence
 and truth;
On that very night he left her to her anguish and
 her ruth.

 * * * * * * * * *

Far he wandered to a country wherein no man knew
 his name.
For ten weary years he dwelt there, nursing still his
 wrath and shame.

Then his haughty heart grew softer, and he thought
 by night and day
Of the bride he had deserted, till he hardly dared
 to pray—

Thought of her, a spotless maiden, fair and beautiful and good;
Thought of his relentless anger that had cursed her womanhood;

Till his yearning grief and penitence at last were all complete,
And he longed, with bitter longing, just to fall down at her feet.

* * * * * * * * *

Ah! how throbbed his heart when, after many a weary day and night,
Rose his native towers before him, with the sunset glow alight!

Through the gates into the city on he pressed with eager tread;
There he met a long procession — mourners following the dead.

"Now why weep ye so, good people? and whom bury ye to-day?

Why do yonder sorrowing maidens scatter flowers along the way?

"Has some saint gone up to Heaven?" "Yes," they answered, weeping sore:
"For the Organ-Builder's saintly wife our eyes shall see no more;

"And because her days were given to the service of God's poor,
From His church we mean to bury her. See! yonder is the door."

No one knew him; no one wondered when he cried out, white with pain;
No one questioned when, with pallid lips, he poured his tears like rain.

"'T is some one whom she has comforted who mourns with us," they said,
As he made his way unchallengèd, and bore the coffin's head.

Bore it through the open portal, bore it up the echoing aisle,
Set it down before the altar, where the lights burned clear the while:

When, oh, hark! the wondrous organ of itself began to play
Strains of rare, unearthly sweetness never heard until that day!

All the vaulted arches rang with the music sweet and clear;
All the air was filled with glory, as of angels hovering near;

And ere yet the strain was ended, he who bore the coffin's head,
With the smile of one forgiven, gently sank beside it — dead.

They who raised the body knew him, and they laid him by his bride;

Down the aisle and o'er the threshold they were carried side by side;

While the organ played a dirge that no man ever heard before,
And then softly sank to silence—silence kept for evermore.

AT DAWN.

At dawn when the jubilant morning broke,
   And its glory flooded the mountain side,
I said, " 'T is eleven years to-day,
   Eleven years since my darling died!"

And then I turned to my household ways,
   To my daily tasks, without, within,
As happily busy all the day
   As if my darling had never been!—

As if she had never lived, or died!
   Yet when they buried her out of my sight,
I thought the sun had gone down at noon,
   And the day could never again be bright.

Ah, well! As the swift years come and go,
   It will not be long ere I shall lie

AT DAWN.

Somewhere under a bit of turf,
   With my pale hands folded quietly.

And then some one who has loved me well—
   Perhaps the one who has loved me best—
Will say of me as I said of her,
   "She has been just so many years at rest,"—

Then turn to the living loves again,
   To the busy life, without, within,
And the day will go on from dawn to dusk,
   Even as if I had never been!

Dear hearts! dear hearts! It must still be so!
   The roses will bloom, and the stars will shine,
And the soft green grass creep still and slow,
   Sometime over a grave of mine—

And over the grave in your hearts as well!
   Ye cannot hinder it if ye would;
And I—ah! I shall be wiser then—
   I would not hinder it if I could!

KING IVAN'S OATH.

King Ivan ruled a mighty land
Girt by the sea on either hand;
A goodly land as e'er the sun
In its long journey looked upon!
His knights were loyal, brave, and true,
Eager their lord's behests to do;
His counselors were wise and just,
Nor ever failed his kingly-trust;
The nations praised him, and the state
Grew powerful, and rich, and great;
While still with long and loud acclaim,
His people hailed their monarch's name!

Fronting the east, a stately pile,
The palace caught the sun's first smile;
Lightly its domes and arches sprung,
As earth's glad hills when earth was young;

And, miracles of airy grace,
Each tower and turret soared in space.
Within —— But here no rhythmic flow
Of words with light and warmth aglow
Can tell the story. Not more fair
Are your own castles hung in air!
Painter and sculptor there had wrought
The utmost beauty of their thought;
There the rich fruit of Persian looms
Glowed darkly bright as tropic blooms;
There fell the light like golden mist,
Filtered through clouds of amethyst;
There bright-winged birds and odorous flowers
With song and fragrance filled the hours;
There Pleasure flung the portals wide,
And soul and sense were satisfied!

The queen? No fairer face than hers
E'er smiled upon its worshipers;
And she was good as fair, 't was said,
And loved the king ere they were wed.
And he? No doubt he loved her, too,

After a kingly fashion — knew
She had a right his throne to share,
And would be mother of his heir.
But yet, to do him justice, he
Sometimes forgot his royalty, —
Forgot his kingly crown, and then
Loved, and made love, like other men!

There seemed no shadow near the throne;
Yet oft the great king walked alone,
Hands clasped behind him, head bowed down,
And on his royal face a frown.
Sat Mordecai within his gate?
What scoffing specter mocked his state?
What demon held him in a spell?
Alas! the sweet queen knew too well!
Apples of Sodom ate he, since
She had not borne to him a prince,
Though thrice his hope had budded fair,
And he had counted on an heir.
Three little daughters, dainty girls
With sunshine tangled in their curls,

Bloomed in the palace; but no son—
The long-expected, waited one,
Flower of the state, and pride of all—
Grew at the king's side, straight and tall!

The king was angered. It may be
No worse than other men was he;
But—a high tower upon a hill—
His light shone far for good or ill!
In from the chase one day he rode;
To the queen's chamber fierce he strode;
Where, bending o'er her 'broidery frame,
Her pale cheeks burned with sudden flame
At his quick coming. Up she rose,
Stirred from her wonted calm repose,
A lily flushing when the sun
Its stately beauty looked upon!
Alas! alas! so blind was he,
Or else he did not care to see—
He had no pity, though she stood
In perfect flower of womanhood!
"You bear to me no son," he said;

Then flinging back his haughty head:
"Each base-born peasant has an heir,
His name to keep, his crust to share,
While I — the king of this broad land —
Have no son near my throne to stand!
Who, then, shall reign when I am dead?
Who wield the scepter in my stead?
Inherit all my pride and power,
And wear my glory as his dower?
Give me a man-child, who shall be
Lord of the realm, himself, and me!"

Then pallid lips made slow reply, —
"God ordereth. Not you nor I!"

His brow flushed hot; a sudden clang
As of arms throughout the chamber rang,
And turning on his heel, he threw
Back wrathful answer: "That may do
For puling women — not for me!
Now, by my good sword, we shall see!
So help me Heaven, I will not brook

On a girl's face again to look!
And when you next shall bear a child,
Though fair a babe as ever smiled,
If it be not a princely heir,
By all the immortal gods, I swear
I ne'er will speak to it, nor break
My soul's stern silence for Love's sake!"

Then forth he fared and rode away,
Nor saw the queen again that day:—
The hapless queen, who to the floor
Sank prone and breathless, as the door
Swung to behind him, and his tread
Down the long arches echoèd.
In truth she was in sorry plight
When her maids found her late that night,
The king learned that which spoiled his rest,
But kept the secret in his breast!

   *   *   *   *   *   *   *   *

At length, when months had duly sped,
High streamed the banners overhead,
And all the bells rang out at morn

In jubilant peals—a Prince was born!
Now let the joyous music ring!
Now let the merry minstrels sing!
Now pour the wine and crown the feast
With fruits and flowers of all the East!
Now let the votive candles shine
And garlands bloom on every shrine!
Now let the young, with flying feet
Time to bewildering music beat,
And let the old their joys rehearse
In stirring tale, or flowing verse!
Now fill with shouts the waiting air,
And scatter largess everywhere!

Ah! who so happy as the king?
Swift flew the hours on eager wing;
And the boy grew apace, until
The second summer, sweet and still,
Dropped roses round him as he played
Where arched the leafy colonnade.
How fair he was tongue cannot say,
But he was fairer than the day!

And never princely coronet
On brow of nobler mold was set;
Nor ever did its jewels gleam
Above an eye of brighter beam!
And never yet where sunshine falls,
Flooding with light the cottage walls,
'Mid hum of bee, or song of birds,
Or tenderest breath of loving words,
Blossomed a sweeter child than he!
How the king joyed his strength to see,
Counting the weeks that flew so fast—
Each fuller, happier than the last!
Six months had passed since he could walk;
Was it not time the prince should talk?
Ah! baby words with tripping feet!
Ah! baby laughter, silver sweet!

At length within the palace rose
Rumor so strange that friends and foes
Forgot their love, forgot their hate,
Pausing to croon and speculate.
Vague whispers floated in the air;

A hint of mystery here and there;
A sudden hush, a startled glance,
Quick silences and looks askance.
Thus day by day the wonder grew,
Till o'er the kingdom wide it flew.
The prince — his father — what was this
Strange tale so surely told amiss?
The young prince dumb? Who dared to say
That nature such a prank could play?
Dumb to the king? In silence bound,
With voiceless lips that gave no sound
When the king questioned? — Yet no lute,
Nor chiming bell, nor silver flute,
Nor lark's song, high in ether hung,
Rang clearer than the prince's tongue!

The court physicians came and went;
Learned men from all the continent
Gave wise opinions, talked of laws,
Stroked their gray beards, nor found the cause.
Then bribes were tried, and threats. The child,
As one bewildered, sighed and smiled,

In a wild storm of weeping broke,
Moved its red lips, but never spoke.

The changeful years rolled on apace;
The young prince wore a bearded face;
The good queen died; the king grew gray;
A generation passed away.
Courtiers forgot to tell the tale;
Gossip itself grew old and stale.
But never once, in all the years
That bore such freight of joys and tears,
Was the spell broken: not one word
From son to sire was ever heard.
Mutely his father's face he scanned—
Mutely he clasped his agèd hand—
Mutely he kissed him when at last
To death's long slumber forth he passed!
Come weal or woe, he could not break
The mystic silence for Love's sake!

IN MEMORIAM.

[Cyrus M. and Mary Ripley Fisher, lost on Steamship Atlantic, April 1st, 1873.]

ONCE, long ago, with trembling lips I sung
   Of one who, when the earliest flowers were seen,
So sweet, so dear, so beautiful and young,
   Came home to sleep where kindred graves were green.

Soft was the turf we raised to give her room;
   Clear were the rain-drops, shining as they fell;
Sweet the arbutus, with its tender bloom
   Brightening the couch of her who loved it well.

Yet, in our blindness, how we wept that day,
   When the earth fell upon her coffin-lid!
O, ye belovèd whom I sing *this* day,
   Could we but know where your dear forms lie hid!

Could we but lay you down by her dear side,
    Wrapped in the garments of eternal rest,
Where the still hours in slow succession glide,
    And not a dream may stir the pulseless breast—

Where all day long the shadows come and go,
    And soft winds murmur and sweet song-birds sing—
Where all night long the star-light's tender glow
    Falls where the flowers you loved are blossoming—

Then should the tempest of our grief grow calm;
    Then moaning gales should vex our souls no more;
And the clear swelling of our thankful psalm
    Should drown the beat of surges on the shore.

But the deep sea will not give up its dead.
    O, ye who know where your belovèd sleep,
Bid heart's-ease bloom on each love-guarded bed,
    And bless your God for graves whereon to weep!

WEAVING THE WEB.

"This morn I will weave my web," she said,
   As she stood by her loom in the rosy light,
And her young eyes, hopefully glad and clear,
   Followed afar the swallow's flight.
"As soon as the day's first tasks are done,
   While yet I am fresh and strong," said she,
"I will hasten to weave the beautiful web
   Whose pattern is known to none but me!

"I will weave it fine, I will weave it fair,
   And ah! how the colors will glow!" she said;
"So fadeless and strong will I weave my web
   That perhaps it will live after I am dead."
But the morning hours sped on apace;
   The air grew sweet with the breath of June;
And young Love hid by the waiting loom,
   Tangling the threads as he hummed a tune.

"Ah, life is so rich and full!" she cried,
  "And morn is short though the days are long!
This noon I will weave my beautiful web,
  I will weave it carefully, fine and strong."
But the sun rode high in the cloudless sky;
  The burden and heat of the day she bore
And hither and thither she came and went,
  While the loom stood still as it stood before.

"Ah! life is too busy at noon," she said;
  "My web must wait till the eventide,
Till the common work of the day is done,
  And my heart grows calm in the silence wide."
So, one by one, the hours passed on
  Till the creeping shadows had longer grown;
Till the house was still, and the breezes slept,
  And her singing birds to their nests had flown.

"And now I will weave my web," she said,
  As she turned to her loom ere set of sun,
And laid her hand on the shining threads
  To set them in order one by one.

But hand was tired, and heart was weak:
  "I am not as strong as I was," sighed she,
"And the pattern is blurred, and the colors rare
  Are not so bright, or so fair to see!

"I must wait, I think, till another morn;
  I must go to my rest with my work undone;
It is growing too dark to weave!" she cried,
  As lower and lower sank the sun.
She dropped the shuttle; the loom stood still;
  The weaver slept in the twilight gray.
Dear heart! Will she weave her beautiful web
  In the golden light of a longer day?

RABBI BENAIAH.

Rabbi Benaiah at the close of day,
   When the low sun athwart the level sands
   Shot his long arrows, from far Eastern lands
Homeward across the desert bent his way.

Behind him trailed the lengthening caravan,—
   The slow, weird camels, with monotonous pace;
   Before him, lifted in the clear, far space,
From east to west the towers of his city ran!

Impatiently he scanned the darkening sky;
   Then girding in hot haste, "What ho!" cried he,
   "Bring the swift steed Abdallah unto me!
As rode his Bedouin master, so will I!"

Soon like a bird across the waste he flew,
   Nor drew his rein till at the massive gate

That guards the citadel's supremest state
He paused a moment, slowly entering through.

Then down the shadowy, moonlit streets he sped;
   The city slept; but like a burning star,
   Where his own turret-chamber rose afar,
A clear, strong light its steady radiance shed!

Into his court he rode with sudden clang.
   The startled slaves bowed low, but spake no word;
   By no quick tumult was the midnight stirred,
No shouts of welcome on the night air rang!

But with slow footsteps down the turret-stairs,
   With trembling lips that did but breathe his name,
   And sad, averted eyes, his fair wife came,—
The lady Judith,—wan with tears and prayers.

Then swift he cried out, less in wrath than fear,
   "Now, by my beard! is this the way ye keep
   My welcome home? Go wake my sons from sleep,
And let their glad tongues break the silence here!"

"Not so, my dear lord! Let them rest," she said.
  "Young eyes need slumber. But come thou with
    me.
I have a trouble to make known to thee
Ere I before thee can lift up my head."

Into an inner chamber led she him,
  And with her own hands brought him meat and
    wine,
  A purple robe, and linen pure and fine.
He half forgot that her sweet eyes were dim!

"Now for thy trouble!" cried he, laughing loud.
  "Hast torn thy kirtle? Are thy pearls astray?
  What! Tears? My camels o'er yon desert way
Bring treasures that had made Queen Esther
    proud!"

Slowly she spake, nor in his face looked she.
  "My lord, long years ago a friend of mine
  Left with me jewels, costly, rare, and fine,
Bidding me guard them carefully till he

"Again should call for them. The other day
  He sent his messenger. But I have learned
  To hold them as my own! Have I not earned
A right to keep them? Speak, my lord, I pray!"

"Strange sense of honor hath a woman's heart!"
  The rabbi answered hotly. "Now, good lack!
  Where are the jewels? I will send them back
Ere yet the sun upon his course may start!

"Show me the jewels!" Up she rose as white
  As any ghost, and mutely led the way
  Into the turret-chamber whence the ray
Seen from afar had blessed the rabbi's sight.

And with slow, trembling hands she drew aside
  The silken curtain from before the bed
  Whereon, in snowy calm, their boys lay dead.
"There are the jewels, O, my lord!" she cried.

A CHILD'S THOUGHT.

Softly fell the twilight;
   In the glowing west
Purple splendors faded;
   Birds had gone to rest;
All the winds were sleeping;
   One lone whip-poor-will
Made the silence deeper,
   Calling from the hill.

Little Fred,—the darling,—
   On his mother's knee,
In the gathering darkness,
   Still as still could be,
Watched the deepening shadows;
   Saw the stars come out;
Saw the weird bats flitting
   Stealthily about;

A CHILD'S THOUGHT.

Saw across the river
   How the furnace glow,
Like a fiery pennant,
   Wavered to and fro:
Saw the tall trees standing
   Black against the sky,
And the moon's pale crescent
   Swinging far and high.

Deeper grew the darkness;
   Darker grew his eyes
As he gazed around him,
   In a still surprise.
Then he listened, listened!
   "What is this I hear
All the time, dear mamma,
   Sounding in my ear?"

"I hear nothing," said she,
   "All the earth is still."
But he listened, listened,
   With an eager will,

Till at length a quick smile
   O'er the child-face broke,
And a kindling luster
   In his dark eyes woke.

" Now I know, dear mamma!
   I can hear the sound
Of the wheels, the great wheels
   That move the world around!"
Oh, ears earth has dulled not!
   In your purer sphere,
Strains from ours withholden
   Are you wise to hear?

"GOD KNOWS."

Oh! wild and dark was the winter night
   When the emigrant ship went down,
But just outside of the harbor bar,
   In the sight of the startled town.
The winds howled, and the sea roared,
   And never a soul could sleep,
Save the little ones on their mothers' breasts,
   Too young to watch and weep.

No boat could live in the angry surf,
   No rope could reach the land:
There were bold, brave hearts upon the shore,
   There was many a ready hand,—

"GOD KNOWS."

Women who prayed, and men who strove
  When prayers and work were vain;
For the sun rose over the awful void
  And the silence of the main.

All day the watchers paced the sands,
  All day they scanned the deep,
All night the booming minute-guns
  Echoed from steep to steep.
"Give up thy dead, O cruel sea!"
  They cried athwart the space;
But only a baby's fragile form
  Escaped from its stern embrace.

Only one little child of all
  Who with the ship went down
That night when the happy babies slept
  So warm in the sheltered town.
Wrapped in the glow of the morning light,
  It lay on the shifting sand,
As fair as a sculptor's marble dream,
  With a shell in its dimpled hand.

There were none to tell of its race or kin.
  "God knoweth," the pastor said,
When the sobbing children crowded to ask
  The name of the baby dead.
And so, when they laid it away at last
  In the church-yard's hushed repose,
They raised a stone at the baby's head,
  With the carven words, "God knows."

UNSOLVED.

'T is the old unanswered question! Since the stars together sung
In the glory of the morning, when the earth was fair and young,

Man hath asked it o'er and over, of the heavens so far and high,
And from out the mystic silence never voice hath made reply!

Yet again to-night I ask it, though I know, O friend of mine,
There will come, to all my asking, never answering voice of thine.

Ah! how many times the grasses have grown green above thy grave,

And how many times above it have we heard the
  cold winds rave !

Thou hast solved the eternal problem that the ages
  hold in fee ;
Thou dost know what we but dream of; where we
  marvel, thou dost see.

What is truth, and what is fable; what the prophets
  saw who trod
In their rapt, ecstatic visions up the holy mount of
  God !

Not of these high themes I question — but O friend,
  I fain would know
How beyond the silent river all the long years come
  and go !

Where they are, our well-belovèd, who have vanished
  from our sight,
As the stars fade out of heaven at the dawning of
  the light;

How they live and how they love there, in the
 "somewhere" of our dreams;
In the "city lying four-square" by the everlasting
 streams!

Oh, the mystery of being! Which is better, life or
 death?
Thou hast tried them both, O comrade, yet thy
 voice ne'er answereth!

Hast thou grown as grow the angels? Doth thy
 spirit still aspire
As the flame that soareth upward, mounting higher
 still, and higher?

In the flush of early manhood all thy earthly days
 were done;
Short thy struggle and endeavor ere the peace of
 heaven was won.

But for us who stayed behind thee—oh! our hands
 are dark with toil,

And upon our souls, it may be, are the stains of
    earthly moil.

Hast thou kept the lofty beauty and the glory of
    thy youth?
Dost thou see our temples whitening, smiling softly
    in thy ruth?

But for us — we bear the burdens that you dropped
    so long ago,
And the cares you have forgotten, and the pains you
    missed, we know.

Yet — the question still remaineth! Which is better,
    death or life?
The not doing, or the doing? Joy of calm, or joy
    of strife?

Which is better — to be saved from temptation and
    from sin,
Or to wrestle with the dragon and the glorious fight
    to win?

Ah! we know not, but God knoweth! All resolves
    itself to this,—
That He gave to us the warfare, and to thee the
    heavenly bliss.

It was best for thee to go hence in the morning of
    the day;
Till the evening shadows lengthen it is best for us
    to stay!

FIVE.

"But a week is so long!" he said,
   With a toss of his curly head.
"One, two, three, four, five, six, seven!—
Seven whole days! Why, in six you know
(You said it yourself—you told me so)
The great GOD up in heaven
Made all the earth and the seas and skies,
The trees and the birds and the butterflies!
How can I wait for my seeds to grow?"

"But a month is so long!" he said,
   With a droop of his boyish head.
"Hear me count—one, two, three, four—
Four whole weeks, and three days more;
Thirty-one days, and each will creep
As the shadows crawl over yonder steep.
Thirty-one nights, and I shall lie

Watching the stars climb up the sky!
How can I wait till a month is o'er?"

"But a year is so long!" he said,
  Uplifting his bright young head.
"All the seasons must come and go
Over the hills with footsteps slow—
Autumn and Winter, Summer and Spring;
Oh, for a bridge of gold to fling
Over the chasm deep and wide,
That I might cross to the other side,
Where she is waiting—my love, my bride!"

"Ten years may be long," he said,
  Slow raising his stately head,
"But there's much to win, there is much to lose;
A man must labor, a man must choose,
And he must be strong to wait!
The years may be long, but who would wear
The crown of honor, must do and dare!
No time has he to toy with fate
Who would climb to manhood's high estate!"

"Ah! life is not long!" he said,
  Bowing his grand white head.
"One, two, three, four, five, six, seven!
Seven times ten are seventy.
Seventy years! as swift their flight
As swallows cleaving the morning light,
Or golden gleams at even.
Life is short as a summer night—
How long, O GOD! is eternity?"

QUIETNESS.

I would be quiet, Lord,
  Nor tease, nor fret;
Not one small need of mine
  Wilt Thou forget.

I am not wise to know
  What most I need;
I dare not cry too loud
  Lest Thou shouldst heed:

Lest Thou at length shouldst say,
  " Child, have thy will;
As thou hast chosen, lo!
  Thy cup I fill!"

What I most crave, perchance
  Thou wilt withhold,

QUIETNESS.

As we from hands unmeet
   Keep pearls, or gold;

As we, when childish hands
   Would play with fire,
Withhold the burning goal
   Of their desire.

Yet choose Thou for me—Thou
   Who knowest best;
This one short prayer of mine
   Holds all the rest!

WINTER.

O my roses, lying underneath the snow!
Do you still remember summer's warmth and glow?
Do you thrill, remembering how your blushes burned
When the Day-god on you ardent glances turned?

Great tree, wildly stretching bare arms up to heaven,
Do you think how softly, on some warm June even,
All your young leaves whispered, all your birds sang low,
As with rhythmic motion boughs swayed to and fro?

River, lying whitely in a frozen sleep,
Know you how your pulses used to throb and leap?
How you danced and sparkled on your happy way,
In the summer mornings when the world was gay?

Dear Earth, dumbly waiting God's appointed time,
Are you faint with longing for the voice sublime?
Wrapped in stony silence, does your great heart beat,
Listening in the darkness for the coming of His feet?

THE "CHRISTUS" OF THE PASSION PLAY OF OBERAMMERGAU.

How does life seem to thee? I long to look
Into thine inmost soul, and see if thou
Art even as other men! Oh, set apart
And consecrate so long to purpose high,
Canst thou take up again our common lot,
And live as we live? Canst thou buy and sell,
Stoop to small needs, and petty ministries,
Work and get gain, eat, drink, and soundly sleep,
Sin and repent, as these thy brethren do?
Unto what name less sacred answerest thou
Who hast been called the Christ of Nazareth?
Thou who hast worn the awful crown of thorns,
Hanging like Him upon the dreadful Tree,
Canst thou, uncrowned, forget thy royalty?

THE MOUNTAIN ROAD.

Only a glimpse of mountain road
That followed where a river flowed;
Only a glimpse—then on we passed
Skirting the forest dim and vast

I closed my eyes. On rushed the train
Into the dark, then out again,
Startling the song-birds as it flew
The wild ravines and gorges through.

But, heeding not the dangerous way
O'erhung by sheer cliffs, rough and gray,
I only saw, as in a dream,
The road beside the mountain stream.

No smoke curled upward in the air,
No meadow-lands stretched broad and fair;

THE MOUNTAIN ROAD.

But towering peaks rose far and high,
Piercing the clear, untroubled sky.

Yet down the yellow, winding road
That followed where the river flowed,
I saw a long procession pass
As shadows over bending grass.

The young, the old, the sad, the gay,
Whose feet had worn that narrow way,
Since first within the dusky glade
Some Indian lover wooed his maid;

Or silent crept from tree to tree —
Spirit of stealthy vengeance, he!
Or breathless crouched while through the brake
The wild deer stole his thirst to slake.

The barefoot school-boys rushing out
An eager, crowding, roisterous rout;
The sturdy lads; the lassies gay
As bobolinks in merry May;

The farmer whistling to his team
When first the dawn begins to gleam;
The loaded wains that one by one
Drag slowly home at set of sun;

Young lovers straying hand in hand
Within a fair, enchanted land;
And many a bride with lingering feet;
And many a matron calm and sweet;

And many an old man bent with pain;
And many a solemn funeral train;
And sometimes, red against the sky,
An army's banners waving high!

All mysteries of life and death
To which the spirit answereth,
Are thine, O lonely mountain road,
That followed where the river flowed!

ENTERING IN.

The church was dim and silent
  With the hush before the prayer,
Only the solemn trembling
  Of the organ stirred the air;
Without, the sweet, still sunshine;
  Within, the holy calm
Where priest and people waited
  For the swelling of the psalm.

Slowly the door swung open,
  And a little baby girl,
Brown-eyed, with brown hair falling
  In many a wavy curl,

With soft cheeks flushing hotly,
   Shy glances downward thrown,
And small hands clasped before her,
   Stood in the aisle alone.

Stood half abashed, half frightened
   Unknowing where to go,
While like a wind-rocked flower,
   Her form swayed to and fro,
And the changing color fluttered
   In the little troubled face,
As from side to side she wavered
   With a mute, imploring grace.

It was but for a moment;
   What wonder that we smiled,
By such a strange, sweet picture
   From holy thoughts beguiled?
Then up rose some one softly;
   And many an eye grew dim,
As through the tender silence
   He bore the child with him.

And I—I wondered (losing
   The sermon and the prayer)
If when sometime I enter
   The "many mansions" fair,
And stand, abashed and drooping,
   In the portal's golden glow,
Our God will send an angel
   To show me where to go!

THE DIFFERENCE.

Only a week ago and thou wert here!
   I touched thy hand, I saw thy dear, dark eyes,
I kissed thy tender lips, I felt thee near,
   I spake, and listened to thy low replies.

To-day what leagues between us! Hill and vale,
   The rolling prairies and the mighty seas;
Gray forest reaches where the wild winds wail,
   And mountain crests uplifted to the breeze!

So far thou art, who wert of late so near!
   The stars we watched have changed not in the skies;
Still do thy hyacinth bells their beauty wear,
   Yet half a continent between us lies!

But swift as thought along the "singing wires"
   There flies a message like a bright-winged bird—
"All 's well! All 's well!" and ne'er from woodland choirs
   By gladder music hath the air been stirred!

   *   *   *   *   *   *   *   *

But thou, O thou, who but a week ago,
   Passed calmly out beyond our yearning gaze,
As some grand ship all solemnly and slow
   Sails out of sight beyond the gathering haze—

Oh, where art *thou?* In what far distant realm,
   What star in yon resplendent fields of light,
On what fair isle that no rude seas may whelm,
   Dost thou, O brother, find thy home to-night?

Or art thou near us? There are those who say
   That but a breath divides our world from thine;
A little cloud that may be blown away—
   A gossamer veil than spider's web more fine.

THE DIFFERENCE.

Dost thou, a shadowy presence, linger near
    Thine own loved haunts, the paths thou wert wont to tread,
Where woods were still, and shining brooks ran clear,
    And waving boughs arched greenly overhead?

Oh! be thou far or near, it is the same!
    From thee there floats no message thro' the air;
No glad "All 's well" comes to us in thy name
    That we the joy of thy new life may share!

THOU KNOWEST.

Thou knowest, O my Father! Why should I
    Weary high heaven with restless prayers and tears?
Thou knowest all! My heart's unuttered cry
    Hath soared beyond the stars and reached Thine ears.

Thou knowest — ah, Thou knowest! Then what need,
    O, loving God, to tell Thee o'er and o'er,
And with persistent iteration plead
    As one who crieth at some closèd door?

"Tease not!" we mothers to our children say, —
    "Our wiser love will grant whate'er is best."
Shall we, Thy children, run to Thee alway,
    Begging for this and that in wild unrest?

I dare not clamor at the heavenly gate,
    Lest I should lose the high, sweet strains within;
O, Love Divine! I can but stand and wait
    Till Perfect Wisdom bids me enter in!

A FLOWER FOR THE DEAD.

You placed this flower in her hand, you say?
This pure, pale rose in her hand of clay?
Methinks could she lift her sealèd eyes
They would meet your own with a grieved surprise!

She has been your wife for many a year,
When clouds hung low and when skies were clear;
At your feet she laid her life's glad spring,
And her summer's glorious blossoming.

Her whole heart went with the hand you won;
If its warm love waned as the years went on,
If it chilled in the grasp of an icy spell,
What was the reason? I pray you tell!

You cannot? I can; and beside her bier
My soul must speak and your soul must hear.

A FLOWER FOR THE DEAD.

If she was not all that she might have been,
Hers was the sorrow, yours the sin.

Whose was the fault if she did not grow
Like a rose in the summer? Do you know?
Does a lily grow when its leaves are chilled?
Does it bloom when its root is winter-killed?

For a little while, when you first were wed,
Your love was like sunshine round her shed;
Then a something crept between you two,
You led where she could not follow you.

With a man's firm tread you went and came;
You lived for wealth, for power, for fame;
Shut in to her woman's work and ways,
She heard the nation chant your praise.

But ah! you had dropped her hand the while;
What time had you for a kiss, a smile?
You two, with the same roof overhead,
Were as far apart as the sundered dead!

You, in your manhood's strength and prime;
She, worn and faded before her time.
'T is a common story. This rose, you say,
You laid in her pallid hand to-day?

When did you give her a flower before?
Ah, well!—What matter when all is o'er?
Yet stay a moment; you 'll wed again.
I mean no reproach; 't is the way of men.

But I pray you think when some fairer face
Shines like a star from her wonted place,
That love will starve if it is not fed;
That true hearts pray for their daily bread.

A RED ROSE.

O Rose, my red, red Rose,
   Where has thy beauty fled?
Low in the west is a sea of fire,
But the great white moon soars high and higher,
   As my garden walks I tread.

Thy white rose-sisters gleam
   Like stars in the darkening sky;
They bend their brows with a sudden thrill
To the kiss of the night-dews soft and still,
   When the warm south wind floats by.

And the stately lilies stand
   Fair in the silvery light,
Like saintly vestals, pale in prayer;
Their pure breath sanctifies the air,
   As its fragrance fills the night.

But O, my red, red Rose!
  My Rose with the crimson lips!
So bright thou wert in the sunny morn,
Yet now thou art hiding all forlorn,
  And thy soul is in drear eclipse!

Dost thou mourn thy lover dead—
  Thy lover, the lordly Sun?
Didst thou see him sink in the glowing west?
With pomp of banners above his rest?
  He shall rise again, sweet one!

He shall rise with his eye of fire—
  And thy passionate heart shall beat,
And thy radiant blushes burn again,
With the joy of rapture after pain
  At the coming of his feet!

MY BIRTHDAY.

My birthday!—" How many years ago?
   Twenty or thirty?" Don't ask me!
" Forty or fifty?"—How can I tell?
   I do not remember my birth, you see!

It is hearsay evidence—nothing more!
   Once on a time, the legends say,
A girl was born—and that girl was I.
   How can I vouch for the truth, I pray?

I know I am here, but when I came
   Let some one wiser than I am tell!
Did this sweet flower you plucked for me
   Know when its bud began to swell?

How old am I? You ought to know
   Without any telling of mine, my dear!

For when I came to this happy earth
  Were you not waiting for me here?

A dark-eyed boy on the northern hills,
  Chasing the hours with flying feet,
Did you not know your wife was born,
  By a subtile prescience, faint yet sweet?

Did never a breath from the south-land come
  With sunshine laden and rare perfume
To lift your hair with a soft caress,
  And waken your heart to richer bloom?

Not one? O mystery strange as life!—
  To think that we who are now so dear
Were once in our dreams so far apart,
  Nor cared if the other were far or near!

But—how old am I? You must tell.
  Just as old as I seem to you!
Nor shall I a day older be
  While life remaineth and love is true!

TWENTY-ONE.

GROWN to man's stature! O my little child!
    My bird that sought the skies so long ago!
My fair, sweet blossom, pure and undefiled,
    How have the years flown since we laid thee low!

What have they been to thee? If thou wert here
    Standing beside thy brothers, tall and fair,
With bearded lip, and dark eyes shining clear,
    And glints of summer sunshine in thy hair,

I should look up into thy face and say,
    Wavering, perhaps, between a tear and smile,
"O my sweet son, thou art a man to-day!"—
    And thou wouldst stoop to kiss my lips the while.

But—up in heaven—how is it with thee, dear?
    Art thou a man—to man's full stature grown?

Dost thou count time as we do, year by year?
    And what of all earth's changes hast thou known?

Thou hadst not learned to love me. Didst thou take
    Any small germ of love to heaven with thee,
That thou hast watched and nurtured for my sake,
    Waiting till I its perfect flower may see?

What is it to have lived in heaven always?
    To have no memory of pain or sin?
Ne'er to have known in all the calm, bright days,
    The jar and fret of earth's discordant din?

Thy brothers—they are mortal—they must tread
    Ofttimes in rough, hard ways, with bleeding feet;
Must fight with dragons, must bewail their dead,
    And fierce Apollyon face to face must meet.

I, who would give my very life for theirs,
    I cannot save them from earth's pain or loss;
I cannot shield them from its griefs or cares;
    Each human heart must bear alone its cross!

Was God, then, kinder unto thee than them,
  O thou whose little life was but a span?
Ah, think it not! In all his diadem
  No star shines brighter than the kingly man,

Who nobly earns whatever crown he wears,
  Who grandly conquers, or as grandly dies;
And the white banner of his manhood bears,
  Through all the years uplifted to the skies!

What lofty pæans shall the victor greet!
  What crown resplendent for his brow be fit!
O child, if earthly life be bitter-sweet,
  Hast thou not something missed in missing it?

THOMAS MOORE.

May 28, 1779–1879.

Hush!—O be ye silent, all ye birds of May!
Cease the high, clear trilling of your roundelay
Be the merry minstrels mute in vale, on hill,
And in every tree-top let the song be still!

O ye winds, breathe softly! Let your voices die
In a low, faint whisper, sweet as love's first sigh;
O ye zephyrs, blowing over beds of flowers,
Be ye still as dews are in the starry hours!

O ye laughing waters, leaping here and there,
Filling with sweet clamor all the summer air,
Can ye not be quiet? Hush, ye mountain streams,
Dancing to glad music from the world of dreams!

And thou, mighty ocean, beating on the shore,
Bid thy angry billows stay their thunderous roar!
O ye waves, lapse softly, in such slumberous calm
As ye know when circling isles of crested palm!

Bells in tower and steeple, be ye mute to-day
As the bell-flowers rocking in the winds of May!
Cease awhile, ye minstrels, though your notes be clear
As the strains that soar in heaven's high atmosphere!

Earth, bid all thy children hearken,—for a voice,
Sweeter than a seraph's, bids their hearts rejoice;
Floating down the silence of a hundred years,
Lo! its deathless music thrills our listening ears!

'T is the one our fathers loved so long ago,
The same songs it taught them warbling clear and low;—
Hark, "Ye Disconsolate!" while the voice so pure
Sings—"Earth has no sorrow that heaven cannot cure!"

Sings of love's wild rapture triumphing o'er pain,
Glorying in giving, counting loss but gain;
Sings the warrior's passion and the patriot's pride.
And the brave, unshrinking, who for glory died;—

Sings of Erin smiling through a mist of tears;
Of her patient waiting all the weary years;
Sings the pain of parting, and the joy divine
When the bliss of meeting stirs the heart like wine;—

Sings of memories waking in "the stilly night";
Of the "young dreams" fading in the morning light;
Of the "rose of summer" perishing too soon;
Of the early splendors waning ere the noon!

O thou tender singer! All the air to-day
Trembles with the burden of thy "farewell" lay;
Crowns and thrones may crumble, into darkness hurled,
Yet is song immortal; song shall rule the world!

SINGING IN THE DARK.

O YE little warblers, flying fast and far
From the balmy south-land, where the roses are,
Robins red and blue-birds, do ye faint to see
How the chill snow-blossoms whiten shrub and tree?

Through the snowy valley cold the north winds sweep;
Mother Earth, half-wakened, turns again to sleep;
Silent lies the river in an icy trance,
And the frozen meadows wait the sun's hot glance.

Dull and gray the skies are. Soft and blue were those
That so late above you bent at daylight's close;
Do ye grieve, remembering all the balm and bloom,
All the warmth and sweetness of the starlit gloom?

Do ye sadly wonder what strange impulse drew
All your flashing pinions the far ether through?
Do ye count it madness that so wide ye strayed
From the starry jasmine and the orange shade?

Yet this morn I heard ye singing in the dark,
Songs of such rare sweetness that the world might hark!
O ye blessed minstrels, silent not for pain,
God is in the heavens, and your sun shall shine again!

TWO SONNETS.

I.

When I awake at morn, refreshed, renewed,
  Glad with the gladness of the jocund day
  And jubilant with all the birds of May,
My spirit shrinks from Night's dull quietude.
With it and Sleep I have a deadly feud.
  I hear the young winds in the maples play,
  The river singing on its happy way,
The swallows twittering to their callow brood.
The fresh, fair earth is full of joyous life;
  The tree-tops toss in billowy unrest;
    The very mountain shadows are astir!
With eager heart I thrill to join the strife;
  Doing, not dreaming, to my soul seems best,
    And I am lordly Day's true worshiper!

II.

But when with Day's long weariness oppressed,
  With folded hands I watch the sun go down,
  Lighting far torches in the steepled town,
And kindling all the glowing, reddening west;
When every sleepy bird has sought its nest;
  When the long shadows from the hills are thrown,
  And Night's soft airs about the world are blown,
Thou heart of mine, how sweet it is to rest!
O, Israfil! Thou of the tuneful voice!
  It will be night-fall when thy voice I hear,
    Summoning me to slumber soft and low!
Day will be done. Then will I not rejoice
  That all my tasks are o'er and rest is near,
    And, like a tired child, be glad to go?

TO ZÜLMA.

I.

Sometimes my heart grows faint with longing, dear, —
  Longing to see thy face, to touch thy hand.
  But mountains rise between us; leagues of land
Stretch on and on where mighty lakes lie clear
In the far spaces, and great forests rear
  Their somber crowns on many a lonely strand!
  Yet, O my fair child, canst thou understand,
Thou whose dear place was once beside me here,
How yet I dare not pray that thou and I
  Again may dwell together as of old?
    There is a gate between us, locked and barred,
Over which we may not climb, and standing nigh
  Is the white angel Sorrow, who doth hold
    The only key that may unlock its ward!

II.

Yet think not I would have it otherwise!
   Our God, who knoweth women's hearts, knows best —
And every little bird must build its nest
From whence it soareth, singing, to the skies.
What though the one that thou hast builded lies
   Where sinks the sun to its enchanted rest,
   If, on each breeze that bloweth east or west,
To thee, on swiftest wing, my spirit flies?
We are not far apart, and ne'er shall be!
   For Love, like God, knoweth not time, nor space,
   And it is freer than the viewless air;
And well I know, belovèd, that if we
   Trod different planets in yon starry space
     We should reach out, and find each other there!

MERCÉDÈS.

(June 27th, 1878.)

O FAIR young queen, who liest dead to-day
   In thy proud palace o'er the moaning sea,
   With still, white hands that never more may be
Lifted to pluck life's roses bright with May—
Little is it to you that, far away,
   Where skies you knew not bend above the free,
   Hearts touched with tender pity turn to thee,
And for thy sake a shadow dims the day!
But youth and love and womanhood are one,
   Though across sundering seas their signals fly;
Young Love's pure kiss, the joy but just begun,
   The hope of motherhood, thy people's cry—
   O thou fair child! was it not hard to die
And leave so much beneath the summer sun?

SLEEP.

Who calls thee "gentle Sleep?"—O! rare coquette,
  Who comest crowned with poppies, thou shouldst wear
  Nettles instead, or thistles, in thy hair;
For thou 'rt the veriest elf that ever yet
Made weary mortals sigh and toss and fret!
  Thou dost float softly through the drowsy air
  Hovering as if to kiss my lips and share
My restless pillow; but ere I can set
  My arms to clasp thee, without sign or speech,
  Save one swift, mocking smile thou 'rt out of reach!
Yet, sometime, thou, or one as like to thee
  As sister is to sister, shalt draw near
  With such soft lullabies for my dull ear,
That neither life nor love shall waken me!

TO-DAY.

WHAT dost thou bring to me, O fair To-day,
That comest o'er the mountains with swift feet?
All the young birds make haste thy steps to greet
   And all the dewy roses of the May
   Turn red and white with joy. The breezes play
On their soft harps a welcome low and sweet;
All nature hails thee, glad thy face to meet,
   And owns thy presence in a brighter ray.
But my poor soul distrusts thee! One as fair
   As thou art, O To-day, drew near to me,
Serene and smiling, yet she bade me wear
The sudden sackcloth of a great despair!
O, pitiless! that through the wandering air
   Sent no kind warning of the ill to be!

GRASS-GROWN.

Grass grows at last above all graves, you say?—
   Why, therein lies the sharpest sting of all!
   To think that stars will rise and dews will fall,
Hills flush with purple splendor, soft winds play
Where roses bloom and violets of May,
   Robin to robin in the tree-tops call,
   And all sweet sights and sounds the senses thrall,
Just as they did before that dreadful day!
   Does that bring comfort? Are we glad to know
That our eyes sometime must forget to weep,
   Even as June forgets December's snow?
Over the graves where our belovèd sleep,
   We charge thee, Time, let not the green grass grow,
Nor your relentless mosses coldly creep!

AT THE TOMB.

O, Soul! rememberest thou how Mary went
  In the gray dawn to weep beside the tomb
  Where one she loved lay buried? Through the
    gloom,
Pallid with pain, and with long anguish spent,
Still pressed she on with solemn, high intent,
  Bearing her costly gifts of rare perfume
  And spices odorous with eastern bloom,
Unto the Master's sepulcher! But rent
  Was the great stone from its low door away;
And when she stooped to peer with startled eyes
  Into the dark where slept the pallid clay,
Lo, it was gone! And there in heavenly guise,
  So grandly calm, so fair in morn's first ray,
She found an angel from the upper skies!

AT REST.

"' When Greek meets Greek,' you know," he sadly said,
 "'Then comes the tug of war.' I deem him great,
 And own him wise and good. Yet adverse fate
Hath made us enemies. If I were dead,
And buried deep with grave-mold on my head,
 I still believe, that, came he soon or late
 Where I was lying in my last estate,
My dust would quiver at his lightest tread!"
 The slow years passed; and one fair summer night,
When the low sun was reddening all the west,
 I saw two grave-mounds, where the grass was bright,
Lying so near each other that the crest
 Of the same wave touched each with amber light.
But, ah, dear hearts! how undisturbed their rest!

F. A. F.

When upon eyes long dim, to whom the light
   Of sun and stars had unfamiliar grown,—
     Eyes that so long in deepening shades had known
The mystic visions of the inner sight,—
Day broke, at last, after the weary night,
   I cannot think its sudden glory shone
In pitiless brightness, dazzling, clear, and white—
   A piercing splendor on the darkness thrown!
Softly as moonlight steals upon the skies,
   Slowly as shadows creep at set of sun,
     Gently as falls a mother's tender kiss,
So softly stole the light upon his eyes;
   So slowly passed the shadows one by one;
     So gently dawned the morning of his bliss!

TOO WIDE!

O MIGHTY Earth, thou art too wide, too wide!
   Too vast thy continents, too broad thy seas,
   Too far thy prairies stretching fair as these
Now reddening in the sunset's crimson tide!
Sundered by thee how have thy children cried
   Each to some other, until every breeze
   Has borne a burden of fond messages
That all unheard in thy lone wastes have died!
Draw closer, O dear Earth, thy hills that soar
   Up to blue skies such countless leagues apart!
   Bid thou thine awful spaces smaller grow!
Compass thy billows with a narrower shore,
   That yearning lips may meet, heart beat to heart,
   And parted souls forget their lonely woe!

RESURGAMUS.

What though we sleep a thousand leagues apart,
  I by my mountains, you beside your sea?
  What though our moss-grown graves divided be
By the wide reaches of a continent's heart?
When from long slumber we at length shall start
  Wakened to stronger life, exultant, free,
  This mortal clothed in immortality,
Where shall I find my heaven save where thou art?
Straight as a bird that hasteth to its nest,
  Glad as an eagle soaring to the light,
    Swift as the thought that bears my soul to thine
When yon lone star hangs trembling in the west,
  So straight, so glad, so swift to thee my flight,
    Led on through farthest space by love divine!

IN KING'S CHAPEL.

(BOSTON, NOV. 3, 1878.)

O, LORD OF HOSTS, how sacred is this place,
  Where, though the tides of time resistless flow,
  And the long generations come and go,
Thou still abidest! In this holy space
The very airs are hushed before Thy face,
  And wait in reverent calm, as voices low
  Blend in the prayers and chantings, soft and slow,
And the gray twilight stealeth on apace.
Hark! There are whispers from the time-worn walls;
  The mighty dead glide up the shadowy aisle;
  And there are rustlings as of angels' wings
While from the choir the heavenly music falls!
  Well may we bow in grateful praise the while —
    In the King's Chapel reigns the King of Kings!

THY NAME.

What matters it what men may call Thee, Thou,
  The Eternal One, who reign'st supreme, alone,
  The boundless universe Thy mighty throne?
When souls before Thee reverently bow,
Oh, carest Thou what name the lips breathe low
  Jove, or Osiris, or the God Unknown
  To whom the Athenians raised their altar stone,
Or Thine, O Holiest, unto whom we vow?
The sun hath many names in many lands;
  Yet upon all its golden splendors fall,
    Where'er, from age to age entreating still,
The adoring earth uplifts its waiting hands.
  Love knows all names and answereth to all—
    Who worships Thee may call Thee what he will!

THREE DAYS.

I.

What shall I bring to lay upon thy bier
   O Yesterday! thou day forever dead?
   With what strange garlands shall I crown thy head,
Thou silent One?—For rose and rue are near
Which thou thyself didst bring me; heart's-ease clear
   And dark in purple opulence that shed
   Rare odors round—worm-wood, and herbs that fed
My soul with bitterness—they all are here!
When to the banquet I was called by thee
   Thou gavest me rags and royal robes to wear;
   Honey and aloes mingled in the cup
Of costly wine that thou didst pour for me;
   Thy throne, thy footstool, thou didst bid me share;
   On crusts and heavenly manna bade me sup!

II.

Thou art no dreamer, O, thou stern To-day!
  The dead past had its dreams; the real is thine.
  An armored knight, in panoply divine,
It is not thine to loiter by the way,
Though all the meads with summer flowers be gay,
  Though birds sing for thee, and though fair stars shine,
  And every god pours for thee life's best wine!
Nor friend nor foe hath strength to bid thee stay.
Gleaming beneath thy brows with smoldering fire
  Thine eyes look out upon the eternal hills
    As forth thou ridest with thy spear in rest.
From the far heights a voice cries, "Come up higher!"
  And in swift answer all thy being thrills,
    When lo! 't is night—thy sun is in the west!

III.

But thou, To-morrow! never yet was born
  In earth's dull atmosphere a thing so fair—
  Never yet tripped, with footsteps light as air,
So glad a vision o'er the hills of morn!
Fresh as the radiant dawning,—all unworn
  By lightest touch of sorrow, or of care,
  Thou dost the glory of the morning share
By snowy wings of hope and faith upborne!
O, fair To-morrow! what our souls have missed
  Art thou not keeping for us, somewhere, still?
    The buds of promise that have never blown—
  The tender lips that we have never kissed—
    The song whose high, sweet strain eludes our skill—
      The one white pearl that life hath never known!

VERMONT.

(WRITTEN FOR THE VERMONT CENTENNIAL CELEBRATION, AT BENNINGTON, AUGUST 15, 1877.)

I.

O, WOMAN-FORM, majestic, strong and fair,
Sitting enthronèd where in upper air
Thy mountain-peaks in solemn grandeur rise,
Piercing the splendor of the summer skies,—
Vermont! Our mighty mother, crowned to-day
    In all the glory of thine hundred years,
If thou dost bid me sing, how can I but obey?
What though the lips may tremble, and the verse
That fain would grandly thy grand deeds rehearse
May trip and falter, and the stammering tongue
Leave all unrhymed the rhymes that should be sung?
I can but do thy bidding, as is meet,
Bowing in humble homage at thy feet—
Thy royal feet—and if my words are weak,
O crownèd one, 't was thou didst bid me speak!

II.

Yet what is there to say,
Even on this proud day,
This day of days, that hath not oft been said?
What song is there to sing
That hath not oft been sung?
What laurel can we bring,
That Ages have not hung
A thousand times above their glorious dead?
What crown to crown the living
Is left us for our giving,
That is not shaped to other brows,
That wore it long ago?
Our very vows but echo vows
Breathed centuries ago!
Earth has no choral strain,
No sweet or sad refrain,
No lofty pæan swelling loud and clear,
That Virgil did not know,
Or Dante, wandering slow
In mystic trances, did not pause to hear!

When gods from high Olympus came
To touch old Homer's lips with flame,
The morning stars together sung
To teach their raptures to his tongue.
For him the lonely ocean moaned;
For him the mighty winds intoned
Their deep-voiced chantings, and for him
Sweet flower-bells pealed in forests dim.
From earth and sea and sky he caught
The spell of their divinest thought,
While yet it blossomed fresh and new
As Eden's rosebuds wet with dew!
Oh! to have lived when earth was young,
With all its melodies unsung!
The dome of Heaven bent nearer then
When gods and angels talked with men,—
When Song itself was newly born,
The Incarnation of the Morn!
But now, alas! all thought is old,
All life is but a story told,
And poet-tongues are manifold;
And he is bold who tries to wake

Even for God, or Country's sake,
In voice, or pen, or lute, or lyre,
Sparks of the old Promethean fire!

III.

AND yet,—O Earth, thank God!—the soul of song
　Is as immortal as the eternal stars!
O, trembling heart! take courage and be strong.
　Hark! to a voice from yonder crystal bars:—

" Did the roses blow last June ?
　　Do the stars still rise and set ?
And over the crests of the mountains
　　Are the light clouds floating yet ?
Do the rivers run to the sea
　　With a deep, resistless flow ?
Do the little birds sing north and south
　　As the seasons come and go ?

" Are the hills as fair as of old ?
　　Are the skies as blue and far ?

Have you lost the pomp of the sunset,
  Or the light of the evening star?
Has the glory gone from the morning?
  Do the wild winds wail no more?
Is there now no thunder of billows
  Beating the storm-lashed shore?

" Is Love a forgotten story?
  Is Passion a jester's theme?
Has Valor thrown down its armor?
  Is Honor an idle dream?
Is there no pure trust in woman?
  No conquering faith in God?
Are there no feet strong to follow
  In the paths the martyrs trod?

" Did you find no hero graves
  When your violets bloomed last May—
Prouder than those of Marathon,
  Or 'old Platea's day'?
When your red and white and blue
  On the free winds fluttered out,

Were there no strong hearts and voices
  To receive it with a shout?
  Oh! let the Earth grow old?
  And the burning stars grow cold!
  And, if you will, declare man's story told!
Yet, pure as faith is pure,
And sure as death is sure,
As long as love shall live, shall song endure!"

IV.

WHEN one by one the stately, silent Years
  Glide like pale ghosts beyond our yearning sight,
  Vainly we stretch our arms to stay their flight,
  So soon, so swift, they pass to endless night!
    We hardly learn to name them,
    To praise them, or to blame them,
    To know their shadowy faces,
    Ere we see their empty places!
    Only once the glad Spring greets them;
    Only once fair Summer meets them;
    Only once the Autumn glory

Tells for them its mystic story;
Only once the Winter hoary
Weaves for them its robes of light!
Years leave their work half done; like men, alas!
With sheaves ungathered to their graves they pass,
And are forgotten. What they strive to do
Lives for a while in memory of a few;
Then over all Oblivion's waters flow—
The Years are buried in the Long Ago!
But when a Century dies, what room is there for tears?
Rather in solemn exaltation let us come,
      With roll of drum
      (Not muffled as in woe),
With blare of bugles, and the liquid flow
Of silver clarions, and the long appeal
Of the clear trumpets ringing peal on peal
With clash of bells, and hosts in proud array
To pay meet homage to its burial day!
For its proud work is done. Its name is writ
Where all the ages that come after it
Shall read the eternal letters, blazoned high
On the blue dome of the impartial sky.

What ruthless fate can darken its renown,
  Or dim the luster of its starry crown?
On mountain-peaks of Time each Century stands
    alone;
And each, for glory or for shame, hath reaped what
    it hath sown!

v.

But this—the one that gave thee birth
A hundred years ago, O beauteous mother!
This mighty century had a mightier brother,
  Who from the watching earth
Passed but last year! Twin-born indeed were they,—
For what are twelve months to the womb of time
Pregnant with ages?—Hand in hand they climbed
With clear, young eyes uplifted to the stars,
With great, strong souls that never stopped for bars,
Through storm and darkness up to glorious day!
Each knew the other's need; each in his breast
The subtle tie of closest kin confessed;
Counted the other's honor as his own;
Nor feared to sit upon a separate throne;

Nor loved each other less when — wondrous fate! —
One gave a Nation life, and one a State!

VI.

OH! rude the cradle in which each was rocked, —
  The infant Nation, and the infant State!
Rough nurses were the Centuries, that mocked
At mother-kisses, and for mother-arms
Gave their young nurslings sudden harsh alarms,
Quick blows and stern rebuffs. They bade them wait,
Often in cold and hunger, while the feast
Was spread for others, and, though last not least,
Gave them sharp swords for playthings, and the din
Of actual battle for the mimic strife
  That childhood glories in!
Yet not the less they loved them. Spartans they
Who could not rear a weak, effeminate brood.
Better the forest's awful solitude,
Better the desert spaces, where the day
Wanders from dawn to dusk and finds no life!

VII.

But over all the tireless years swept on,
  Till side by side the Centuries grew old,
  And the young Nation, great and strong and bold,
Forgot its early struggles, in triumphs later won!
  It stretched its arms from East to West;
  It gathered to its mighty breast
  From every clime, from every soil,
  The hunted sons of want and toil;
  It gave to each a dwelling-place;
  It blent them in one common race;
  And over all, from sea to sea,
  Wide flew the banner of the free!
  It did not fear the wrath of kings,
  Nor the dread grip of deadlier things—
  Gaunt Famine with its ghastly horde,
  Dishonor sheathing its foul sword,
  Nor faithless friend, nor treacherous blow
  Struck in the dark by stealthy foe;
  For over all its wide domain,
  From shore to shore, from main to main,

From vale to mountain-top, it saw
The reign of plenty, peace, and law!

VIII.

THUS fared the Nation, prosperous, great, and free,
Prophet and herald of the good to be;
And on its humbler way, in calm content,
The lesser State, the while, serenely went.
Safe in her mountain fastnesses she dwelt,
Her life's first cares forgot, its woes unfelt,
And thought her bitterest tears had all been shed,
For peace was in her borders, and God reigned overhead.

IX.

BUT suddenly over the hills there came
A cry that rent her with grief and shame—
A cry from the Nation in sore distress,
Stricken down in the pride of its mightiness!
With passionate ardor up she sprang,
And her voice like the peal of a trumpet rang,

"What ho! what ho! brave sons of mine,
Strong with the strength of the mountain pine!
To the front of the battle, away! away!
The Nation is bleeding in deadly fray,
The Nation, it may be, is dying to-day!
On, then, to the rescue! away! away!"

X.

Ah! how they answered let the ages tell,
For they shall guard the sacred story well!
Green grows the grass, to-day, on many a battle-field;
War's dread alarms are o'er; its scars are healed;
Its bitter agony has found surcease;
A re-united land clasps hands in peace.
But, oh! ye blessèd dead, whose graves are strown
From where our forests make perpetual moan,
To those far shores where smiling Southern seas
Give back soft murmurs to the fragrant breeze,—
Oh! ye who drained for us the bitter cup,
Think ye we can forget what ye have offered up?
The years will come and go, and other centuries die,

And generation after generation lie
Down in the dust; but long as stars shall shine,
Long as Vermont's green hills shall bear the pine,
As long as Killington shall proudly lift
Its lofty peak above the storm-cloud's rift,
Or Mansfield hail the blue, o'erarching skies,
Or fair Mount Anthony in grandeur rise,
So long shall live the deeds that ye have done,
So deathless be the glory ye have won!

XI.

Not with exultant joy
And pride without alloy,
Did the twin Centuries rejoice when all was o'er.
What though the Nation rose
Triumphant o'er its foes?
What though the State had gained
The meed of faith unstained?
Their mighty hearts remembered the dead that came
no more!
Remembered all the losses,
The weary, weary crosses,

Remembered earth was poorer for the blood that
 had been shed,
And knew that it was sadder for the story it had
 read!
  So clasping hands with somewhat saddened mien,
  And eyes uplifted to the Great Unseen
  That rules alike o'er Centuries and men,
  Onward they walked serenely towards—the End!

XII.

ONE reached it last year. Ye remember well
The wondrous tale there is no need to tell—
How the whole world bowed down beside its bier,
How all the Nations came, from far or near,
Heaping their treasures on its mighty pall—
Never had kingliest king such funeral!
Old Asia rose, and girding her in haste,
Swept in her jeweled robes across the waste,
And called to Egypt lying prone and hid
Where waits the Sphinx beside the pyramid;
Fair Europe came with overflowing hands,

Bearing the riches of her many lands;
Dark Afric, laden with her virgin gold,
Yet laden deeper with her woes untold;
Japan and China in grotesque array,
And all the enchanted islands of Cathay!

XIII.

To-day the other dies.
It walked in humbler guise,
Nor stood where all men's eyes
    Were fixed upon it.
Earth may not pause to lay
  A wreath upon its bier,
Nor the world heed to-day
  Our dead that lieth here!
Yet well they loved each other —
It and its greater brother.
To loftiest stature grown,
Each earned its own renown;
Each sought of Time a crown,
    And each has won it.

XIV.

But what to us are Centuries dead,
And rolling Years forever fled,
Compared with thee, O grand and fair
    Vermont—our goddess-mother?
Strong with the strength of thy verdant hills,
Fresh with the freshness of mountain-rills,
Pure as the breath of the fragrant pine,
Glad with the gladness of youth divine,
Serenely thou sittest throned to-day
Where the free winds that round thee play
Rejoice in thy waves of sun-bright hair,
    O thou, our glorious mother!
Rejoice in thy beautiful strength and say,
    Earth holds not such another!
Thou art not old with thy hundred years,
Nor worn with toil, or care, or tears;
But all the glow of the summer time
Is thine to-day in thy glorious prime!
Thy brow is fair as the winter snows,
With a stately calm in its still repose;

While the breath of the rose the wild bee sips
Half-mad with joy, cannot eclipse
The marvelous sweetness of thy lips;
And the deepest blue of the laughing skies
Hides in the depths of thy fearless eyes,
Gazing afar over land and sea
Wherever thy wandering children be!
Fold on fold,
Over thy form of grandest mold,
Floweth thy robe of forest green,
Now light, now dark, in its emerald sheen.
Its broidered hem is of wild flowers rare,
With feathery fern-fronds light as air
Fringing its borders. In thy hair
Sprays of the pink arbutus twine,
And the curling rings of the wild grape vine.
Thy girdle is woven of silver streams;
Its clasp with the opaline luster gleams
Of a lake asleep in the sunset beams;
And, half concealing
And half revealing,
Floats over all a veil of mist
Pale tinted with rose and amethyst!

XV.

Rise up, O noble mother of great sons,
Worthy to rank among earth's mightiest ones,
And daughters fair and beautiful and good,
Yet wise and strong in loftiest womanhood,—
Rise from thy throne, and standing far and high
Outlined against the blue, adoring sky,
Lift up thy voice, and stretch thy loving hands
In benediction o'er these waiting lands!
Take thou our fealty! at thy feet we bow,
Glad to renew each oft-repeated vow!
No costly gifts we bring to thee to-day;
No votive wreaths upon thy shrine we lay;
Take thou our hearts, then!—hearts that fain would be
From this day forth, O goddess, worthier thee!

A LAST WORD.

Where will it go to reach thine ears?
   My father, thou dost wear
Somewhere beyond the stars to-night
   Thy crown of silver hair.

Somewhere thou *art*. No wandering ghost
   In vast, vague realms of space—
But thine own self, majestic, fair,
   In thine appointed place.

By one long look thy soul replied
   When last I cried to thee,
As thou wert drifting out of sight
   Upon the unknown sea;

And well I know that thou wouldst turn
   Even from joys divine,

A LAST WORD.

If but thy listening ears could hear
   One faltering word of mine.

Yet, knowing this, I cannot lay
   My book upon thy knee,
Saying, "O father, once again
   I bring my sheaves to thee!"

www.ingramcontent.com/pod-product-compliance
Lightning Source LLC
Chambersburg PA
CBHW030434190426
43202CB00036B/211